WILLIAM WALTON

FAÇADE

First and Second Suites for Orchestra

STUDY SCORE

EDITED BY

DAVID LLOYD-JONES

MUSIC DEPARTMENT

OXFORD

UNIVERSITY PRESS

OXFORD
UNIVERSITY PRESS

Great Clarendon Street, Oxford OX2 6DP,
United Kingdom

Oxford University Press is a department of the University of Oxford.
It furthers the University's objective of excellence in research, scholarship,
and education by publishing worldwide. Oxford is a registered trade mark of
Oxford University Press in the UK and in certain other countries

First published in Volume 18 of the William Walton Edition, 2007
This study score edition first published 2014

Impression: 1

ISBN 978-0-19-340569-1

Music origination by Per Hartmann

Printed by CPI group (UK) Ltd, Croydon CR0 4YY

CONTENTS

PREFACE

Between 1922 and 1928 William Walton set forty-three poems by Edith Sitwell for speaker(s) and instrumental ensemble. After an extended process of rejection and addition, a final tally of twenty-one was established during the 1940's, and these were belatedly published in 1951 to form *Façade: an Entertainment*.

In 1926 Walton chose five numbers—all but one of which featured dance—to form an orchestral suite. This, minus 'Swiss Jodelling Song', was first performed under Walton's direction on 3 December 1926 as an interlude during a Ballets Russes evening at the Lyceum Theatre. Surprise has often been expressed that the selection did not include the most famous *Façade* number, 'Popular Song', but this was because it was not composed until 1928. The Suite was published by Oxford University Press in 1936.

In 1931 Frederick Ashton chose the Suite for his ballet *Façade*, but added 'Scotch Rhapsody' and 'Popular Song', plus the opening 'Fanfare', which Walton agreed that the ballet's conductor, his friend Constant Lambert, could orchestrate. In time 'Country Dance', also scored by Lambert, was added, but Walton himself was responsible for the addition of 'Noche Española' and 'Foxtrot' in the 1940 revival. A Second Orchestral Suite was published in 1938, though no reference was made to the fact that Lambert was responsible for four of the six numbers. John Barbirolli gave the first performance with the New York Philharmonic Orchestra at Carnegie Hall on 30 March 1938.

In 1960 Walton selected seven numbers from both Suites which he and OUP termed the 'Special Suite'. This was the First Suite but with 'Popular Song' and 'Foxtrot' from the Second inserted before the final 'Tarantella'.

DAVID LLOYD-JONES, 2014

A fuller account of the Suites, together with detailed textual notes, can be found in Volume 18 of the William Walton Edition.

FAÇADE

First and Second Suites for Orchestra

FIRST SUITE ORCHESTRATION

PICCOLO (doubling Flute 2)

FLUTE

2 OBOES (second doubling Cor Anglais)

2 CLARINETS

2 BASSOONS

4 HORNS (3 and 4 *ad lib.*)

2 TRUMPETS

TROMBONE

TUBA

TIMPANI

PERCUSSION (3 players: Triangle, Tambourine, Castanets, Rattle, Clashed and Suspended Cymbals, Glockenspiel, Xylophone, Side Drum, Bass Drum)

STRINGS

Duration: 10–11 minutes

Suite No. 1 was first performed as a symphonic interlude (without No. 3) at a performance of the Ballets Russes at the Lyceum Theatre, London, on 3 December 1926. The resident orchestra was conducted by the composer.

Façade: Suite No. 1

I Polka

WILLIAM WALTON

♩ = 116

Piccolo

Flauto

Oboi 1 2

Clarinetti (A) 1 2

Fagotti 1 2

Corni (F) 1 2 ★ 3 4

Trombe (C) 1 2

Trombone

Tuba

Timpani

Percussione

Violini I ♩ = 116

Violini II

Viole

Violoncelli

Contrabassi

★ Horns 3 and 4 ad lib.

Copyright 1936 by Oxford University Press, London. New edition © 2007.

Printed in Great Britain

OXFORD UNIVERSITY PRESS, MUSIC DEPARTMENT, GREAT CLARENDON STREET, OXFORD OX2 6DP

4

5

6

8

II Valse

★ Horns 3 and 4 ad lib.

10

20

marcatissimo

25

28

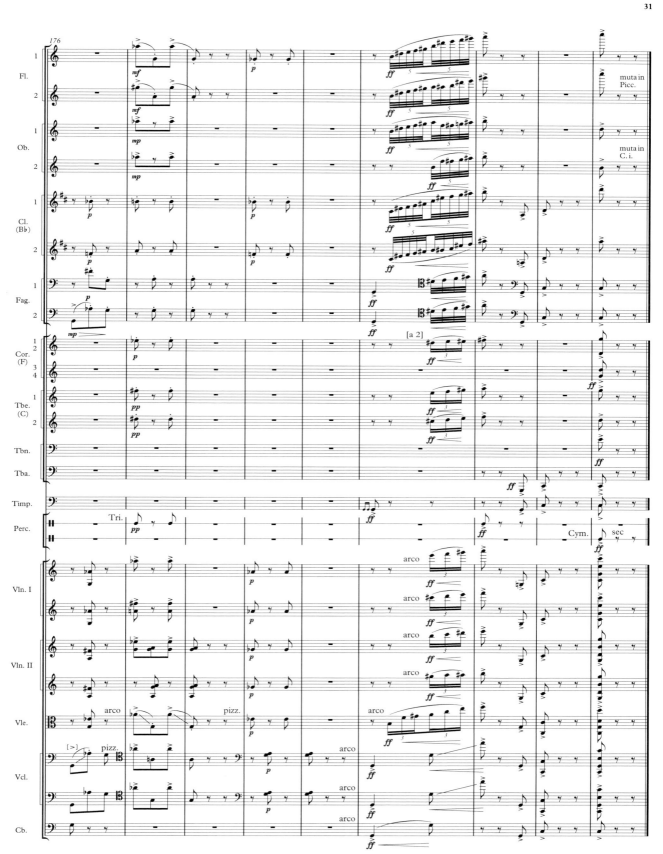

III Swiss Jodelling Song

★ Cymbal struck with the triangle itself, not the triangle stick.

IV Tango – Pasodoblé

★ Horns 3 and 4 ad lib.

42

45

★ For Special Suite, go to 'Popular Song' (p. 106)

V Tarantella Sevillana

★ Horns 3 and 4 ad lib.

52

55

★ See Textual Notes

62

65

SECOND SUITE ORCHESTRATION

PICCOLO (doubling Flute 2)

FLUTE

2 OBOES

COR ANGLAIS or ALTO SAXOPHONE (or, preferably, both)

2 CLARINETS

2 BASSOONS

2 HORNS

2 TRUMPETS

TROMBONE

PERCUSSION (1–2 player(s), preferably with 'traps' for No. VI; Triangle, Tambourine, Castanets, Suspended Cymbal, Wood block, Chinese blocks, Side Drum, Bass Drum)

STRINGS

Duration: 10–11 minutes

Suite No. 2 was first performed (without No. 6) at Carnegie Hall, New York, on 30 March 1938. The New York Philharmonic Orchestra was conducted by John Barbirolli.

The two suites may conveniently be mixed and played as a whole, in which case the following order is recommended:
  (1) Fanfare (II, No. 1)
  (2) Scotch Rhapsody (II, No. 2)
  (3) Valse (I, No. 2)
  (4) Tango–Pasodoblé (I, No. 4)
  (5) Swiss Jodelling Song (I, No. 3)
  (6) Country Dance (II, No. 3)
  (7) Polka (I, No. 1)
  (8) Noche Española (II, No. 4)
  (9) Popular Song (II, No. 5)
(10) Old Sir Faulk (II, No. 6)
(11) Tarantella Sevillana (I, No. 5)

Total duration: 22 minutes

Façade: Suite No. 2

I Fanfare

WILLIAM WALTON

★ Either Cor Anglais or Alto Sax. can be dispensed with in this number if desired.

72

attacca subito No. II

II Scotch Rhapsody

★ The Cor Anglais can be replaced by Alto Sax., but use Cor. Angl. for preference.

★ Between signs ⌐ ⌐ to be played only if there is no Cor Angl. [see Textual Notes]

78

III Country Dance

92

IV Noche Española

★ The Cor Anglais can be replaced by Alto Sax., but use Cor Angl. for preference.

103

106

V Popular Song

★ The Saxophone can be replaced by Cor Anglais, but use Sax. for preference.

110

*) If this movement uses a Corno inglese, the 2nd Bassoon plays these notes.

119

★ For Special Suite, segue 'Old Sir Faulk' over the page.

VI Old Sir Faulk

★ The Saxophone can be replaced by Cor Anglais, but use Sax. for preference.

122

★ Fag. 1 to play (with Cor Anglais) only if no Alto Sax.

123

127

★ For Special Suite, go back to 'Tarantella' (p. 48)